GW01325862

Original title:

Solstice Frost

Author: Olivia Orav

ISBN HARDBACK: 978-9908-52-044-5

ISBN PAPERBACK: 978-9908-52-045-2

ISBN EBOOK: 978-9908-52-046-9

Moonlit Glacier

Under silver skies so bright,
Glaciers gleam in the night.
Whispers of the frozen air,
Dreams and secrets linger there.

Stars above in quiet grace,
Mirror back the icy face.
Each crack a tale from long ago,
In the moonlight's tender glow.

Hushed Serenade of Ice

Softly falls the midnight snow,
Covering the world below.
Silent songs of winter's chill,
Echo in the quiet still.

Beneath the frost, the earth does sigh,
As the chilly winds drift by.
Nature's dance, a subtle art,
Weaving peace into the heart.

Winter's Hallowed Glow

Candles flicker, shadows play,
In the night, the cold holds sway.
Frozen breath hangs in the air,
While the world lies still and bare.

Glow of warmth in hearts so near,
Melts the edges of all fear.
In this hallowed time of grace,
We find beauty in this space.

The Breath of Frozen Ancients

Whispers of the past reside,
In the ice, the tales abide.
Ancient spirits gently roam,
In this place they call their home.

Silent shadows, time stands still,
Memories wrapped in winter's chill.
Glaciers watch as ages flow,
In their depths, the secrets grow.

Celestial Chill

Stars whisper secrets, soft and bright,
The moon paints shadows in the night.
A thin veil of frost on the ground,
In the stillness, magic is found.

Breezes hum ancient songs of old,
As winter's embrace wraps the cold.
Each breath a puff of misty air,
Moments of silence, beauty rare.

Dreams drift like snowflakes from above,
Nature's canvas, a portrait of love.
Under the skies, hearts intertwine,
In this celestial chill, we align.

Hearts Wrapped in White

Winter blankets the earth in white,
With every flake, love takes flight.
Paths covered, stories to unfold,
With every footprint, warmth to hold.

Candles flicker in windows aglow,
The gentle comfort of falling snow.
Together we venture, hand in hand,
In this enchanted, frosted land.

Whispers of love in the frosty air,
Two hearts entwined, a perfect pair.
Wrapped up in blankets, we find delight,
In cozy corners, hearts wrapped in white.

Sunlight's Faded Touch

Golden rays slip behind the trees,
Whispering secrets in the breeze.
Time drips slowly, like molten gold,
A story of warmth, yet untold.

Shadows stretch as daylight wanes,
Carrying echoes of joy and pains.
The sky blushes in a soft embrace,
While stars prepare for their nightly race.

Each sunset a promise, bittersweet,
As daylight falters, moments repeat.
Memories linger in twilight's clutch,
Fading softly, sunlight's touch.

The Art of Frosted Wishes

Icicles hang like dreams of the past,
In the chill, wishes are cast.
Whispers of hope on winter's breath,
Each frost a moment, celebrating death.

Snowflakes dance, pirouetting down,
A flurry of wishes, a delicate crown.
Handwritten notes on frosted glass,
Moments we cherish, fleeting as grass.

In the silence of the snowy night,
Hearts create wishes, pure and bright.
The art of dreaming in every flake,
A canvas of love we create and break.

Shadows in Frosted Glare

In the stillness, shadows creep,
Frosted echoes, secrets keep.
Moonlight casts a silver veil,
Whispers soft, a ghostly trail.

Glistening branches, cold and bare,
Silent sighs fill the frosty air.
Footprints linger on the snow,
Stories shared from long ago.

A shimmering path, where dreams await,
Touched by frost, they hesitate.
Crystals dance in winter's breath,
Life and stillness, whispering death.

Stars like candles, twinkle bright,
Guiding lost souls through the night.
In the darkness, truth unwinds,
Shadows reveal what time unbinds.

Winter's Dance of Light

From dawn's embrace, a shimmer spills,
Frosty air, the silence thrills.
Icicles dangle, crystal bright,
Nature's jewels, a fleeting sight.

With each flake that gently twirls,
The world adorned in white unfurls.
Trees wear coats of icy lace,
In the chill, a warm embrace.

Sunbeams struggle, pierce the gloom,
Bringing life to winter's tomb.
Every shadow finds its grace,
In this dance of light, they trace.

Footsteps echo on the ground,
In the hush, a secret found.
Winter's pulse, a gentle hand,
Carving beauty in the land.

As night descends with stars in dance,
In the frost, we find romance.
Holding tight to moments brief,
Winter's light, a quiet belief.

Parchment of Chill

On parchment white, the frost does lay,
A silent script of winter's play.
Each flake a word, so soft, so clear,
Whispering secrets, cold and dear.

The world adorned in icy lace,
Transforms the earth in frozen grace.
With every breath, a cloudy sigh,
A fleeting moment, drifting by.

Branches glisten, diamonds bright,
In the pale of fleeting light.
Nature's breath, a crystal song,
Echoes where the chill belongs.

Emblems of Winter's Touch

Underneath a mantle white,
Nature sleeps in quiet night.
Each flake, a soft and gentle kiss,
Winter's breath we cannot miss.

Whispers float on frosty air,
Stories linger everywhere.
Footprints faint by glimmering streams,
Jagged paths of fragile dreams.

Trees stand tall, in regal might,
Draped in silver, pure and bright.
An emblem of the cold embrace,
Winter's touch, a fleeting grace.

Glimmering Underworld

Beneath the snow, where shadows sleep,
A glimmering world, secrets keep.
Frosty veins through earth, they creep,
Where ancient whispers softly sweep.

Glowing gems of winter's art,
Crafting beauty from the start.
In stillness lies a magic rare,
A hidden dance beyond compare.

Icicles hang like frozen light,
Crafting dreams in coldest night.
Underworld glimmers bright and clear,
A realm where all the stillness steers.

The Frost's Gentle Hand

The frost arrives with gentle grace,
Painting all with a tender embrace.
A whisper soft, it sweeps the land,
Marking paths with its quiet hand.

Windows framed in icy lace,
Nature dons her frosty face.
Every breath a clouded thread,
In this stillness, dreams are fed.

Stars twinkle in the midnight sky,
While snowy blankets softly lie.
The world wrapped in winter's band,
Held close within the frost's hand.

Frostbitten Echoes

Beneath the moon's pale glow,
Whispers ride the frosty air,
Silent footsteps in the snow,
Memories linger everywhere.

Shadows dance on icy streams,
Gentle night wraps all in white,
Fragrant dreams in frozen beams,
Lingering under stars so bright.

Frozen branches gently sway,
Crackling under winter's breath,
Time seems to pause and play,
In the stillness, life finds depth.

The world a crystal tapestry,
Woven threads of dark and light,
Nature's voice, a reverie,
Sings of warmth despite the night.

A chorus of the cold winds' call,
Echoes through the silent wood,
In the frost, we find it all,
Beauty shines where hardness stood.

Silent Symphony of the Night

The stars above are shining bright,
Wrapped in layers of the night,
Each twinkle tells a story sweet,
In their glow, our hearts will meet.

Softly falls the silent snow,
Cascading down in gentle flow,
Each flake a note in winter's song,
A melody that feels so strong.

The moon, a guardian in the sky,
Watches over as time slips by,
With every breath, we join the tune,
A dance beneath the silver moon.

Whispers of the frozen trees,
Rustle like sweet melodies,
Nature plays her symphony,
In the chill, we find harmony.

As night deepens, peace unfolds,
Wrapped in blankets, warmth beholds,
Together in this calming sight,
We dream beneath the silent night.

Twilight's Icy Caress

Twilight falls, a crimson glow,
Chill descends like whispered sighs,
Night birds sing, and soft winds blow,
Wrapped in evening's cool disguise.

Fingers of frost touch the ground,
As the edges of day blend,
In this hush, no other sound,
Nature's canvas starts to mend.

Each shadow growing ever near,
Embracing us in gentle dreams,
In the dark, we find no fear,
Awash in starlit silver beams.

The sky ablaze with twilight hues,
Painting clouds with shades of pink,
In this moment, we renew,
Bound by time, outside the brink.

A quiet peace descends like snow,
Covering the world so deep,
In the twilight's softening glow,
We find solace, gently sleep.

The Glow of a Winter's Dream

In the quiet of the night,
Snowflakes dance like silent beams,
Wrapped in warmth, a pure delight,
Lost within a winter's dreams.

Candles flicker, shadows play,
Casting shapes upon the walls,
In this light, we drift away,
Hearts aglow as silence calls.

The world outside is veiled in white,
Sparkling under starlit skies,
Each breath we take a soft invite,
To the magic that lies inside.

Whispers float on chilly air,
Stories twined with winter's breath,
In this moment, without care,
We embrace the warmth of depth.

Underneath the moon's embrace,
Love ignites the frosty night,
In this magical, sacred space,
We find our dreams take joyful flight.

Silver Veil of Night

Whispers drift on the cool breeze,
Stars twinkle in the endless skies.
The moon hangs low, a silver tease,
Wrapped in dreams, the world lies.

Soft shadows dance on the ground,
Crickets serenade the dark.
In the silence, peace is found,
The night holds magic, a spark.

Glimmers of light, so tender and bright,
Brush the edges of leaf and stone.
Every moment feels just right,
In this realm where night has grown.

With each breath, the stillness flows,
Embracing hearts without a care.
Underneath the silver glow,
We find solace, sweet and rare.

As dawn approaches, colors blend,
But for now, let the night be.
In this beauty, we transcend,
In the silver veil, we are free.

Luminous Silence

In the hush where shadows play,
Light dances on the edge of night.
Every breath a soft ballet,
In the heart, a spark ignites.

Stars shimmer like distant dreams,
Guiding thoughts with gentle grace.
Moonlight casts its silver beams,
Illuminates this sacred space.

Whispers linger in the dark,
Filling air with tender sighs.
Every silence leaves a mark,
In the quiet, truth belies.

Echoes of the world outside,
Fade away where hopes reside.
In isolation, hearts are tied,
Luminous glow, our trusty guide.

As the dawn begins to break,
Colors bloom in soft embrace.
Yet the silence, I won't forsake,
In its arms, I find my place.

Frosted Dreams in Twilight

As daylight fades to evening's cloak,
The chill wraps round in tender care.
Within the stillness, dreams invoke,
A world transformed, beyond compare.

Each blade of grass, a diamond's glow,
Crystals hung like wishes bright.
In this moment, time moves slow,
Frosty whispers of the night.

Clouds drift softly, painted grey,
While stars awaken in the sky.
Nature sighs in soft display,
As nocturnal creatures lie.

The air is crisp, so fresh, so pure,
Every breath a frosted serenade.
In twilight's grasp, we can endure,
These fleeting dreams that gently fade.

Yet in the cold, warmth we find,
In hearts aglow with joy and peace.
Let frosted dreams, intertwined,
Be cherished close, may they increase.

The Stillness of Long Shadows

As evening falls, the shadows stretch,
Long and lean, they dance with grace.
A quiet world that dreams etch,
In soft embrace, we find our place.

Silence wraps around the trees,
While twilight whispers secrets old.
In every rustle, we can seize,
The stories waiting to be told.

Stars begin their gentle rise,
Painting darkness with their light.
In the calm, the spirit flies,
Finding peace in approaching night.

Time slows down with each slow sigh,
Moments linger, softly flow.
In the stillness, we comply,
With heartbeats, every shadow grows.

So let us bask in evening's glow,
With long shadows at our feet.
Together, we will let them show,
The beauty in the stillness sweet.

Beneath the Crystal Canopy

In shadows soft, where whispers play,
The moonlight weaves a silver ray.
Beneath the boughs where starlights gleam,
We find our hearts in twilight's dream.

A gentle breeze, it calls us near,
With every breath, the night feels clear.
The world, a hush, with magic spun,
As dreams take flight, our souls as one.

Each twinkling star, a tale untold,
In nature's arms, our love unfolds.
With every glance, the heavens sigh,
Beneath the trees, we dare to fly.

So let the night embrace our song,
In this sweet space, we both belong.
Through silver leaves, the secrets weave,
A world below, we still believe.

Frosted Fantasies

A crystal coat on every branch,
Where dreams and truths take a grand chance.
Each flake that falls, a story spun,
In frosted realms where night is done.

The winter air, it wraps us tight,
In glittered whispers of the night.
Together, lost in pure delight,
Our hearts adorned by snowy white.

With every step, the laughter flows,
As world transformed, the magic grows.
In frosty fields, we leap and glide,
With fantasies, our hearts abide.

The silent woods, a blank canvas,
Where every breath feels like a promise.
With dreams anew, we chase the light,
In frosted realms till morning's sight.

When Time Stood Still

A moment caught in golden rays,
Where echoes linger, lost in praise.
With breathless hope, we dared to stay,
In shadows deep, where love would play.

The world around began to fade,
A sacred pause in twilight's shade.
Each heartbeat strong, a ticking clock,
In timeless bliss, we found our rock.

With every glance, the sun would dip,
In sunsets soft, we stole a trip.
With laughter sweet upon the air,
We danced as if without a care.

When time stood still, our hearts entwined,
In worlds unknown, our souls aligned.
A fleeting dream, but love's true call,
In that still moment, we had it all.

Dance of the Crystal Leaves

As autumn fades in hues of gold,
The crystal leaves, a sight so bold.
They twirl and sway on gentle breeze,
A dance of joy among the trees.

In vibrant shades, the world ignites,
With whispers soft of autumn nights.
Each leaf a story, wild and free,
In harmony with all we see.

The laughter echoes through the air,
As nature sings, we join the flare.
With every step, the spirits rise,
In this embrace, no need for guise.

So let us dance beneath the sky,
With every twirl, we learn to fly.
In every rustle, every sigh,
The crystal leaves, our hearts comply.

Glimmers in the Frosted Air

Against the dawn, a shimmer glows,
Each crystal spark in silence flows.
The pines wear coats of powder white,
In stillness dances morning light.

Whispers thread through chilly trees,
A sighing breath, a gentle freeze.
With every glance, the world awakes,
In beauty pure, the stillness breaks.

Glimmers bright on icy streams,
Nature cradles fleeting dreams.
A fleeting hush drapes all around,
In frozen realms, the magic's found.

Barefoot shadows trace the ground,
In the frosted air, a sweet sound.
Echoes soft like tender gifts,
In winter's arms, our spirits lift.

Here, where silence reigns and gleams,
All of life is stitched with seams.
In each fragile, glimmering tear,
We find our love in winter's glare.

Frigid Lullabies of Nature

In twilight's grasp, the cold winds sing,
Notes like snowflakes, they take wing.
Underneath the moon's soft gaze,
Frigid lullabies through the haze.

Crickets hush in midnight's glow,
While shadows dance in silent flow.
The earth slips into soft embrace,
Wrapped in winter's gentle grace.

Branches creak with whispered lore,
As frost paints windows, evermore.
Nature's hush, a calming balm,
In frigid stillness, all is calm.

Stars twinkle like distant dreams,
Reflected in the frozen streams.
Each moment holds a secret deep,
As winter sings the world to sleep.

Wrapped in layers of frosty lace,
The heart finds warmth in nature's space.
In night's embrace, we hold tight,
Frigid lullabies, pure delight.

Echoes of Icy Solitude

In the valley, shadows grow,
Lone figures drift where cold winds blow.
Footsteps crunch on powdered trails,
In the silence, the heart unveils.

Winter skies a muted gray,
Whispers linger, fade away.
In spaces vast, the echoes call,
Echoes of solitude enthrall.

Frosty breath and crisp air sigh,
Underneath the wide, open sky.
Each crack of ice, a voice profound,
In the stillness, solace is found.

Alone, yet not in this vast land,
Nature holds us in her hand.
With every rustle of the trees,
We find companionship in the breeze.

The world, it seems, a dream so clear,
Each icy echo drawing near.
In solitude, we learn to roam,
Finding warmth within the loam.

The Fable of Winter's Kiss

Beneath the breath of winter's sigh,
Soft flurries dance from the sky.
They find the ground, a soft embrace,
A fable spun in time and space.

Branches draped in layers thick,
Nature's magic, a gentle trick.
Each snowflake whispers tales of old,
In every flake, new dreams are told.

The heart beats slow, in sync with night,
As stars emerge, a twinkling sight.
In twilight's arms, dreams softly stir,
The fable breathes in the winter blur.

A kiss from frost, a hush so rare,
Stealing moments, the world laid bare.
In every gleam, a story's hue,
The fable of winter, pure and true.

And when the sun climbs high and bright,
We carry whispers of the night.
Engraved in hearts, with tender bliss,
The timeless tale of winter's kiss.

Ethereal Frostbite

Whispers of the icy night,
Stars twinkle, pure and bright.
Moonlight dances on the ground,
Silent echoes all around.

Biting winds, they softly hum,
Nature's heartbeat, a soft drum.
Frost-kissed branches swaying free,
A stillness wraps the world in glee.

Crystals form on every tree,
A fleeting glimpse of magic's glee.
Time stands still, as hearts take flight,
In the embrace of winter's might.

Footprints trace a fleeting path,
In the quiet, spark the wrath.
But here, in this frozen art,
We find the warmth that lives in heart.

Violet skies begin to glow,
With the essence of the snow.
Wrapped in dreams, the night retreats,
Leaving behind the cold retreats.

Radiant Winter's Lullaby

In the hush of winter's grace,
Snowflakes fall, a soft embrace.
Silent whispers fill the air,
Lullabies without a care.

Fires crackle, warmth inside,
While the world feels cold and wide.
Icicles hang, so crystal clear,
In their beauty, joy draws near.

A blanket white on every hill,
Nature sleeping, peaceful, still.
Dreams take flight in frosty air,
Hearts united, love to share.

Children laugh and spirits soar,
While the seasons offer more.
Joyful moments, laughter bright,
Make the winter feel just right.

As the stars begin to peek,
Gentle winds, they softly speak.
Winter's lullaby enchants,
Awakening the heart that chants.

Echoes in the Snow

Footsteps linger, soft and light,
In the snow, a world so white.
Echoes whisper through the trees,
Carried gently on the breeze.

A melody, both sweet and clear,
Nature's song, the heart draws near.
Branches sway, their tales unfold,
In the hush, a beauty bold.

Clouds drift softly, gray and pale,
While winter weaves her gentle tale.
Echoes dance on frosty air,
In this moment, dreams lay bare.

Frostbite kisses cheeks so red,
While magic thrives in every tread.
Together we embrace the night,
In the glow of soft moonlight.

The quiet speaks, a solemn vow,
That here we live, in essence now.
With every flake, a story grows,
In the gentle echoes of the snow.

The Magic of Crystal Ribbons

Woven light through branches high,
Twinkling stars in a velvet sky.
Crystal ribbons draped with care,
Whispers of the winter air.

Dancing shadows, patterns glisten,
In the night, the heart does listen.
Nature's artwork, bold and free,
Every flake a memory.

Carried forth on chilly streams,
Frosty whispers weave our dreams.
Time stands still with every breath,
Embracing warmth that rises, yet.

Colors fade into twilight's grace,
As sun departs from its embrace.
Nighttime wraps, a gentle shroud,
Breathless beauty, nature proud.

In this dance of light and cold,
Stories of the earth unfold.
On crystal ribbons, we will glide,
Through winter's magic, side by side.

The Tranquil Depths of Cold

In the hush of winter's breath,
Stillness blankets every path,
Whispers float on frosty air,
Nature's calm, a quiet math.

Icicles hang like crystal chains,
Branches draped in silver frost,
Footsteps crunch on snow-clad lanes,
In this beauty, nothing's lost.

Beneath the surface, life can stir,
Hidden warmth, a subtle glow,
Time, it seems, begins to purr,
In the depths, where cold winds blow.

Stars emerge in twilight's choir,
Bright and bold against the night,
Hearts awaken, dreams conspire,
In the dark, there's gentle light.

Winter's peace, a sacred space,
Every flake a work of art,
In their fall, we find our grace,
In the cold, we warm our heart.

Nature's Frozen Lullaby

Softly sings the winter's song,
Snowflakes drift and dance around,
Branches sway, a quiet throng,
In this peace, the world is sound.

Frozen streams, a glistening sheet,
Covering memories untold,
In this stillness, hearts can meet,
In the warmth, the winter's cold.

Whispers of the evening breeze,
Mingle with the pale moonlight,
Nature holds its breath with ease,
In this dream, all feels right.

Echoes of the past resound,
Life beneath the snow persists,
In the silence, hope is found,
Winter's grace, a tender tryst.

As the night wraps all in white,
Stars reflect on dreams aglow,
In the quiet, pure delight,
Nature's lullaby takes hold.

The Art of Winter's Stillness

Upon the ground, a velvet sheet,
Nature's pause in soft embrace,
Each breath drawn in, a rhythmic beat,
Time, it seems, finds slower pace.

Amidst the pines, the stillness reigns,
Every shadow softly cast,
In frozen fields, tranquility gains,
Moments linger, memories last.

Frosted whispers tease the dawn,
As sunlight paints the world anew,
A canvas bright, unmarred, withdrawn,
In the cold, our spirits grew.

Silhouettes in silver gleam,
Dance across the winter's stage,
Birdsongs join the frosty theme,
Nature's peace, we disengage.

In this realm, we find our muse,
Crafting dreams from icy air,
In winter's stillness, we choose,
To savor life, to truly care.

Crystal Shadows Dance

Underneath the waning light,
Shadows weave a tale of grace,
Crystal forms in sparkling sight,
Nature's art, a grand embrace.

Frosted branches, twinkling bright,
Casting patterns on the ground,
In the glow of soft twilight,
Winter's wonder, beauty found.

Evening whispers, secrets shared,
As the night begins to fall,
Each twinkling star is ensnared,
In the silent, frozen call.

The air is crisp, alive with dreams,
Voices of the earth arise,
In shimmering, little streams,
Nature cloaked in frosty ties.

Dancing shadows, nature's trance,
Harmonies of night and snow,
In the stillness, take your chance,
To find the warmth that winter shows.

In the Grip of Glaze

Ice coats the branches, cold and bright,
A shimmering world in the soft moonlight.
Each step is cautious, whispers of dread,
Nature's chill wrapped around my head.

Colors muted, a world held tight,
Footprints echo in the dead of night.
Stillness lingers, time stands still,
In the grip of glaze, the night we fill.

Frost patterns weave on windows' pane,
In this frozen realm, I feel no pain.
A breath of winter in every sigh,
Underneath the starlit sky.

Branches tremble, the wind breathes low,
Glistening rivers through fields of snow.
Captured moments in every glance,
In the grip of glaze, we find our dance.

Shadows stretch as day turns to night,
Guiding us gently, like dreams in flight.
Memories twinkle, frozen in time,
In the grip of glaze, all feels sublime.

Dreaming of Frosted Pines

Nestled deep in the forest's heart,
Glistening jewels, nature's art.
Frosted pines reach for the skies,
A canvas where winter gently lies.

Whispers of silence in the air,
Frost-kissed branches, a beauty rare.
I close my eyes, and there I roam,
In a world where the wild feels like home.

Moonlight dances on sheets of white,
Tales of frost in the soft twilight.
Calmness wraps me like a warm quilt,
In dreams of pines, my worries are stilled.

Every shadow hides a soft sigh,
In this realm where the spirits fly.
Breathless moments, serene and clear,
Dreaming of pines, I hold dear.

Laughter echoes through snowy trails,
Adventure awaits where the light pales.
In winter's embrace, my spirit aligns,
Lost in dreams of frosted pines.

Shadows Flicker in the Cold

Twilight falls, shadows start to play,
In the cold stillness of the day.
Crisp air crackles, whispers in the night,
As frost wraps the world in milky white.

Figures dance in the silver glow,
Life freezes the moments we know.
A gentle hush blankets the ground,
In the stillness, lost echoes abound.

Each breath visible, a puff of mist,
Wrapped in chill, where dreams persist.
Silhouettes shift as the leaves sigh,
Under the frost-laden, starlit sky.

Time meanders through the frozen scene,
Rustling softly where pathways have been.
Flickering shadows draw near and far,
In the chill, we find who we are.

Voices linger in the frozen air,
Stories unfold as we wander unaware.
As echoes fade, the heart grows bold,
In a world where shadows flicker in the cold.

Whispers of the White Wilderness

In the hush of snow, secrets unfold,
Whispers of the wild, stories untold.
Blankets of white over valleys spread,
Nature's lullaby, where dreams are fed.

A hush descends, the world transforms,
Amidst icy trails, the spirit warms.
Glimmers of hope spark through the grey,
In the wilderness, we find our way.

Snowflakes tapping on weary trees,
Carrying tales in the winter breeze.
Frosted paths guide us through the night,
Whispers of wilderness, pure delight.

Under a canopy of shimmering stars,
We tread softly, forgetting our scars.
Each step a promise, each breath a cheer,
In the white wilderness, we conquer fear.

Endless expanse, where freedom lies,
In the snowy landscape, our spirits rise.
As time stands still, stories conspire,
Whispers of the wild, igniting desire.

The Harmony of Chilling Winds

Whispers dance on frosty air,
Leaves rustle with a gentle care.
Moonlit paths where shadows play,
Nature's song at end of day.

Breezes weave a soft embrace,
In the night, we find our place.
Chilling winds that softly sigh,
Tell the tales of passing by.

Stars above, a twinkling choir,
Echo dreams that lift us higher.
With each gust, the world awakes,
In the night, a love that breaks.

Together, souls in sync unite,
Underneath the blanket of night.
Embracing all that whispers near,
In this harmony, we hear.

Endless stories in the breeze,
Carried far with whispered keys.
In chilling winds, hearts align,
Nature's pulse, pure and divine.

When Daylight Takes Flight

Golden rays begin to gleam,
As the night starts to redeem.
Birds take wing, they soar and glide,
In the dawn, we shed our pride.

Colors burst across the sky,
Brushstrokes bold as time goes by.
When daylight spreads its wings so wide,
Hope unfolds, we cannot hide.

Moments dance in vibrant light,
Waking dreams that felt so right.
Every heartbeat, fresh and new,
Promises of life renew.

Clouds dissolve as shadows flee,
In the warmth, we long to be.
When daylight paints with gentle grace,
We find truth in its embrace.

With the sun, our spirits rise,
Chasing clouds in endless skies.
Together, we embrace the flight,
Celebrating life's delight.

Hush of the Shimmering Hour

As the sun begins to sink,
Colors blend, and hearts will link.
Softly glows the evening light,
In this hush, the world feels right.

Silhouettes against the glow,
Whispers meld with ebb and flows.
Stars peek out to join the dance,
In the twilight, take a chance.

The horizon blurs with dreams,
Where nothing's ever as it seems.
In the shimmering hour's grace,
We find peace, a warm embrace.

Time stands still as shadows meet,
In this moment, life's complete.
Hushed tones linger, softly share,
In the night's enchanted air.

In the stillness, love will bloom,
Casting warmth against the gloom.
Hush of night, our spirits entwine,
In the glow, your hand in mine.

Shadows of the Longest Night

Underneath the blanket deep,
Where the darkest secrets sleep.
Silent echoes, whispers low,
In the shadows, feelings grow.

Stars like lanterns dot the sky,
Guiding hearts that learn to fly.
Flickering truths in shadows cast,
Holding tight to dreams amassed.

Moments lost in midnight's clutch,
Every heartbeat bears the touch.
When the longest night prevails,
Starlit paths become our trails.

In the still, a promise lies,
Cloaked in whispers, soft goodbyes.
Shadows whisper truth so clear,
In the night, we have no fear.

Through the dark, we find our way,
In the silence, we will stay.
Shadows weave a tale so bright,
Guiding dreams in longest night.

Winter's Distant Serenade

The snowflakes dance from the sky,
Whispers of winter's lullaby,
Under a blanket, the world sleeps,
In silence, the frosty air keeps.

The fir trees sway with gentle grace,
Holding the chill in their embrace,
Footprints left in the sparkling white,
Marks of joy from a playful night.

A candle flickers in the dark,
Softly shining, a hopeful spark,
As shadows play on the walls near,
Comforting souls with warmth and cheer.

The nightingale dreams in the frost,
Each note of beauty not lost,
While the world slows, it's time to pause,
To feel the stillness, to embrace the cause.

Upon the horizon, stars ignite,
Guiding the heart through the night,
In winter's vast and quiet land,
We find the magic, hand in hand.

Shivers Beneath the Moon

Underneath a silver glow,
Whispers of secrets in the snow,
Chilled winds carry tales untold,
As shadows weave through the cold.

Frost kisses the window's edge,
Nature stands at winter's hedge,
Every breath hangs in the air,
Crafting clouds, delicate and rare.

Moonlight dances on the frozen ground,
Revealing landscapes, profound,
The world adorned in crystal grace,
Hushed as dreams take their place.

In pockets of darkness, spirits roam,
Finding warmth in the coldest home,
While stars shimmer high above,
Kindling hearts with winter love.

From midnight's veil, silence falls,
Echoes through the ancient halls,
Beneath the moon's enchanted sight,
We lose ourselves in the night.

Intricate Patterns of Ice

Frost creates a lace-like design,
Nature's artistry, so divine,
Each crystal tells a fleeting tale,
A masterpiece where shadows pale.

On windows, delicate images form,
Transforming mundane to the warm,
As children press their hands and sigh,
In wonder, they watch the world lie.

The frozen lakes, a mirror bright,
Reflecting stars in silver light,
Nature's canvas stretches wide,
In intricate patterns, beauty hides.

With every breath, the air feels light,
Chill wrapping hearts, taking flight,
Winter's brush paints the world anew,
In shades of white, gray, and blue.

As daylight fades and twilight glows,
Softly the evening's quiet flows,
In frosty air, we find our way,
Through patterns of ice, we softly sway.

Hesitant Sunbeams

The dawn breaks with gentle sighs,
Sunbeams stretching, shyly rise,
Through the mist, they weave and play,
Chasing the shadows of night away.

Clouds whisper in hues of gold,
With stories of warmth that unfold,
While nature awakens from sleep,
In sunlight's grasp, dreams run deep.

Each ray touches frost on the grass,
A glimmering touch that comes to pass,
Awakening life in the stillness,
Hesitant but full of bright thrills.

Birdsong breaks the morning calm,
Every note a sweet, soft balm,
While petals unfurl with delight,
Embracing the soft, warming light.

In the quiet, the world holds its breath,
Each moment savored, life's sweet breadth,
As sunbeams dance on the waking earth,
Celebrating light, love, and rebirth.

A World Adorned in Ice

In the still of winter's breath,
Snowflakes dance like whispered dreams.
A canvas vast, pure and white,
Nature's beauty softly gleams.

Trees wear coats of sparkling frost,
Branches bow beneath their weight.
A hush envelops all around,
In this realm, we contemplate.

Rivers freeze with glassy grace,
Reflections caught in frozen time.
The world seems wrapped in quiet rest,
In this place, a heart can climb.

Mountains stand like silent guards,
With peaks adorned in shining light.
Over valleys, shadows cast,
A dreamland veiled in silver white.

As daylight fades and stars awake,
The moonbeams pulse like gentle sighs.
This world of ice, a tender heart,
Cocooned where warmth and beauty lies.

The Lure of the Icy Horizon

Beyond the ridge where cold winds blow,
Lies a horizon dressed in ice.
A shimmering veil, a world aglow,
Promising secrets, silent and nice.

Footprints trace along the shore,
Where frozen tides embrace the land.
What stories wait behind each door,
In this realm, so pure and grand?

The sun dips low, a fleeting guest,
Painting skies in hues of fire.
Yet every chill feels like a test,
Of heart and spirit's deep desire.

Glistening paths where few have trod,
Lead to realms both vast and wild.
Each breath is crisp, a cool applaud,
Nature's charm, unbeguiled.

With every step, the world expands,
What lies beyond? The whispers call.
The icy horizon, a gift of lands,
Where dreams are born, where hearts enthrall.

Chilling Promises

When the night wraps its icy shroud,
And the stars glimmer like frozen woes,
A promise whispers, soft yet loud,
Of winter's beauty in gentle flows.

Crystal shards in the moonlight gleam,
Nature's bounty, a silver lace.
Frozen rivers weave a dream,
In this chill, we find our place.

Each flake that falls, a tale unfolds,
Of tranquil nights and endless skies.
In frosty arms, the world enfolds,
A magic where the heart complies.

Promises linger in the cold air,
In every breath, a fleeting spark.
A promise of spring beyond despair,
In winter's grasp, we leave our mark.

As dawn ignites, the ice will melt,
Yet memories held in frosted light.
Chilling promises, forever felt,
In the heart of winter's night.

Frosted Reflections

In the glint of morning's fire,
Frosted panes reveal the day.
Seeking warmth, we draw closer,
To the scenes that nature lay.

Each breath a cloud, soft and white,
With laughter echoing in the air.
On this canvas, pure delight,
Moments shared, without a care.

In frozen lakes, reflections gleam,
A mirror of the icy skies.
Wonders caught in a crystal dream,
Where silence speaks and spirit flies.

The stillness wraps us like a shawl,
Embracing joy spun in the cold.
In every flake, a story tall,
Of lives entwined, and hearts consoled.

As day departs and night unfolds,
We cherish these frosted sights.
In our hearts, the warmth beholds,
Reflections bright in winter's nights.

Crystals on Silent Streets

In the hush of night, they gleam,
Tiny jewels in moon's soft stream.
Footsteps whisper on icy ground,
Echoes of dreams where no one is found.

Streetlamps flicker, shadows play,
Casting light on dreams that sway.
Each breath fogs in the chilling air,
A moment caught in the stillness bare.

Silent houses, windows tight,
Guard their warmth from the frosty bite.
Crystals dance on roofs above,
Nature's hand writes tales of love.

Footprints linger, fading light,
In this realm where day meets night.
Outside, the world wears a frosty crown,
As silence drapes its soft, white gown.

Life resumes, but for now, sleep,
In this quiet, secrets keep.
Crystals shimmer where shadows meet,
On these silent, frosted streets.

A Dance of Icy Stars

Night unfolds a silver sheet,
Stars upon the ice do greet.
Shimmers glisten with every sigh,
Beneath a dark, expansive sky.

Whispers swirl in frozen air,
Softly moving without care.
Each flake twirls in a graceful way,
As frost paints night into day.

Galaxies twirl in silent grace,
The universe finds its place.
Icy comets brush the ground,
In this dance, all lost are found.

Hidden dreams in the frosty light,
Glow like jewels in the night.
Each twinkle tells a story old,
In the stillness, secrets unfold.

A ballet under the moon's bright gaze,
Where time lingers, caught in a maze.
The stars, they twine with the ice below,
In a dance only the night can know.

Fragments of a Frozen Dawn

As the night begins to fade,
Light slices through the icy shade.
Each breath mingles with the chill,
Time stands still, a fleeting thrill.

Glistening shards in morning's kiss,
Whisper softly of winter's bliss.
Fragments of dreams, melted away,
In the warmth of the golden ray.

The horizon blushes in pale light,
Chasing shadows, bidding night.
Every crystal begins to thaw,
Revealing beauty in nature's law.

Birds awaken, songs take flight,
Joy spills into the warming night.
With every shimmer, hope is drawn,
In the heart of a frozen dawn.

As day breaks, magic may fade,
But memories linger, unafraid.
In this moment, we stand still,
Frozen fragments time can't kill.

Twilight's Bitter Caress

The sun dips low in twilight's grasp,
A gentle hand, a fleeting clasp.
Golden hues that swiftly drain,
Leaving only twilight's pain.

Shadows creep upon the ground,
Silent whispers, no one around.
In this moment, time suspends,
As daylight's warmth begins to end.

Frost creeps in, a silent thief,
Stealing colors, bringing grief.
Yet in the chill, a beauty lies,
In the crispness of the cold night skies.

Stars emerge with a fragile glow,
Chasing remnants of the sun's show.
Twilight's caress, both sweet and cruel,
In the fading light, we find our rule.

Lingering moments, a bittersweet sigh,
As the world whispers its last goodbye.
Embrace the dusk, let shadows play,
For in twilight, night holds sway.

Frost-kissed Reveries

In the morning light, so bright,
Frost adorns the world in white.
Whispers soft in icy breath,
Nature sleeps, entwined with death.

Trees wear crystals, a sparkling crown,
Silent beauty blankets the town.
Footsteps crunch on paths so clear,
Echoes of winter fill the sphere.

The sun peeks through, a timid glow,
Painting shadows on the snow.
Dreams unfurl in frosted air,
Each sigh carries winter's flair.

Glistening fields, a vast expanse,
Playing with snowflakes, we dance.
Moments captured in frosty grace,
Time sits still in this serene place.

When the night descends, stars align,
Frost-kissed reveries intertwine.
A world enchanted, pure and bright,
Wrapped in the arms of endless night.

A Canvas of Snowflakes

Falling gently from the sky,
Snowflakes dance, a blissful sigh.
Nature's brush, so divine,
Painting dreams, a soft design.

Each flake unique, a wondrous sight,
Whispers of winter, pure delight.
A canvas wide, where silence reigns,
Blankets cover the hills and lanes.

Children laugh in joyful play,
Building wonders through the day.
A snowman stands with a frosty grin,
In this kingdom where dreams begin.

Underneath the moon's pale glow,
A world transformed in a soft show.
With each twirl, a story told,
In frozen beauty, hearts unfold.

As night falls, the magic glows,
A canvas where the stillness grows.
In the chill, our hearts take flight,
In the dance of snowflakes, pure delight.

Crystal Lanterns in the Dark

Twinkling lights in the evening air,
Crystal lanterns casting glare.
The world adorned in silver sheen,
A nighttime wonder, soft and keen.

Branches cloaked in frozen dreams,
Whispering secrets in moonlit beams.
Stars above like diamonds spark,
Guiding souls through the quiet dark.

Fires crackle, warmth surrounds,
In cozy corners, love abounds.
Conversations drift, hearts ignite,
Underneath the crystal light.

Each flicker tells a tale of yore,
A dance of memories, rich and pure.
In the chill, we find our way,
As crystal lanterns light our play.

The night deepens, shadows sway,
But in this glow, we wish to stay.
Heartfelt laughter fills the park,
Beneath the magic, there's a spark.

The Stillness of Winter's Heart

In the hush of winter's breath,
Whispers echo, a dance with death.
Time is still, the world holds tight,
Wrapped in blankets of pure white.

Frosty branches, a silent choir,
In every flake, a hidden fire.
Muffled sounds in the tranquil air,
Nature rests, without a care.

Footprints mark the icy ground,
In this realm where peace is found.
Each moment hangs, a fragile art,
Captured in the stillness of winter's heart.

The sun dips low, shadows grow,
In twilight's grasp, soft winds blow.
Stars emerge in a velvet sky,
In their glow, the world goes shy.

As night unveils its silver sheen,
Dreams take flight in the serene.
In the quiet, we find our part,
In the stillness of winter's heart.

Whispers of Crystal Dreams

In the quiet night we hear,
Softly woven hopes appear.
Fragile visions in the air,
Gently floating, light as hair.

Stars above begin to gleam,
Painting skies of silver dream.
Echoes dance through velvet dark,
Guiding hearts with whispered spark.

Feel the chill of peaceful sighs,
Murmurs sweet as lullabies.
Crystals glimmer, hearts will leap,
In the stillness, memories keep.

Bubbles burst in midnight's grace,
Shadows play and softly trace.
Time stands still, a tender scheme,
Lost in whispers, crystal dream.

As dawn breaks, the visions fade,
Yet in hearts, the dreams are laid.
Carry forth the light's embrace,
In life's journey, find your place.

Moonlight on Ice

Underneath the silver glow,
Frozen lakes begin to show.
Whispers of the night unfold,
Celestial stories told.

Moonbeams dancing on the crest,
Gently lapping with the rest.
Silent echoes in the night,
Painting shadows, pale and bright.

Crystals sparkle, whispers sigh,
Beneath the vast, eternal sky.
In this moment, hearts will race,
Each reflection holds a place.

Breath of winter, crisp and clear,
Every note is close and near.
Harmony of frost and light,
Moonlit magic takes its flight.

As the world begins to freeze,
Nature's art brings hearts to peace.
In this realm of gentle grace,
Moonlight's touch, a warm embrace.

Reflections in the Glare

Glistening waters catch the sun,
Mirrored visions, two in one.
Reflected dreams across the shore,
Echoes of a distant lore.

Silhouettes of memories past,
Floating by, their shadows cast.
Ripples dance in brightest hues,
Whispers carried on the blues.

Caught in sunlight's gentle beam,
Life unfolds like a waking dream.
Fleeting moments blend and bend,
Time is but a faithful friend.

With each glance, a world anew,
Colors shift to shades of blue.
Reflections spark the soul's delight,
In the glare, all feels just right.

As the day begins to wane,
Nature sings a sweet refrain.
In the golden hour's flare,
Hearts are bound in love's own care.

Frosted Whispers of the Woods

Silent trees in winter's breath,
Frosted whispers hide from death.
Nature sleeps, beneath the white,
Secret dreams of soft twilight.

Footsteps quiet on the trail,
Stories woven, ancient tale.
Every branch adorned with lace,
Morning light gives them their grace.

Echoes dance on icy ground,
Lost in stillness, beauty found.
Snowflakes fall like gentle sighs,
Carrying the goodbyes.

Crisp and cold, the world remains,
In its hold, a peace refrains.
Frosted whispers, soft and dear,
Speak to hearts that pause to hear.

As the twilight fades to night,
Winter's cloak, a calming sight.
Within the woods, a sacred space,
Frosted dreams, a cold embrace.

A Breath of Winter's Essence

In the hush of snowflakes, falling light,
Whispers of winter dance through the night.
Bare branches shimmer, cloaked in white,
Nature's breath, a crisp, pure delight.

Silent nights, under a moon's gaze,
Stars sprinkle dreams in a silver haze.
Footsteps crunch on the icy ways,
Time stands still in these tranquil days.

Frosted panes tell tales of old,
Warmth of hearths, stories unfold.
With every gust, the air is bold,
A heartbeat of winter, consider, behold.

Shadows stretch as daylight wanes,
The scent of pine in the chilled veins.
A symphony, where silence reigns,
Winter's essence, tethered in chains.

As dawn breaks, colors softly blend,
The world awakens, nature's blend,
A breath of warmth soon to send,
Embracing life as seasons mend.

Frostbound Enchantment

Frost-laden whispers fill the air,
A frosty enchantment everywhere.
Winds weave magic with chilling flair,
Nature's canvas, pure and rare.

Glistening crystals adorn the ground,
In the silence, a beauty profound.
Frozen echoes in cold surround,
A winter's tale that knows no bound.

Icicles hang like chandeliers bright,
Catch the glimmer of soft moonlight.
In every shadow, in every bite,
Frostbound dreams take elegant flight.

The breath of winter, sharp and clear,
Paints the world with a touch sincere.
Each snowy path brings memories near,
In enchanted moments, we disappear.

As twilight descends, the stars ignite,
Frigid air holds a cozy sight.
Together we roam in the hush of night,
Embracing the magic, hearts get light.

Encounters Under the Ice

Underneath the crystal dome,
Where icy rivers find their home,
Life stirs softly, a hidden tome,
Whispers of secrets, silent roam.

Glimmers of fish dart and swirl,
Through frosted glass, the waters twirl.
In this realm, nature's wonders unfurl,
Beneath the surface, life's gentle whirl.

Fragile patterns of frost align,
Nature's artistry, designs divine.
In quiet moments, we intertwine,
Breath held close, like vintage wine.

A dance of shadows, a story sown,
Encounters rare, in silence grown.
Beneath the ice, the heart has flown,
Secrets shared in the world alone.

As warmth creeps in with the sun's embrace,
The icy surface begins to trace,
Life's new chapter, a vibrant space,
Under the thaw, dreams interlace.

The Glistening Path

A winding path in winter's glow,
With every step, the fresh winds blow.
Footprints spark where silence flows,
The glistening trail of nature's show.

Snowflakes twirl like dancers high,
Under the clean, cerulean sky.
Each crystal glimmers, a soft reply,
To the winter's breath, a soft sigh.

Woodlands dressed in serene white,
Frame the path in pure delight.
Every tree stands tall, a knight,
Guarding secrets of the night.

Echoes of laughter wash the air,
Joy unfolds, freely laid bare.
Gathered warmth, a friendly share,
The glistening path, beyond compare.

As twilight shrouds the world in blue,
A final glance, the heart feels true.
In every moment, memories accrue,
The glistening path leads me to you.

Glacial Melodies at Dusk

Whispers chill as shadows blend,
The sun dips low, a silent friend.
Ice-kissed trees in fading light,
Sing of dusk, of winter's night.

Echoes dance on frozen streams,
Carried forth on twilight dreams.
Anthems hushed by frosty breath,
Nature's voice, defying death.

Stars awaken, shy and bright,
Painting skies with silver light.
In the stillness, beauty grows,
As the icy river flows.

Every flake, a thought expressed,
In the quiet, hearts find rest.
Melodies of frost and sky,
Whisper soft, a lullaby.

Dusk embraces, shadows play,
Adding magic to the gray.
As the world holds its breath tight,
Glacial dreams morph into night.

The Wintering Heartbeat

In the hearth, the embers glow,
Winter's chill begins to flow.
Cradled close, the warmth we find,
Beats of love, against the grind.

Snowflakes swirl, a soft ballet,
Whispered secrets on display.
Each heartbeat, like distant drums,
Through the stillness, softly hums.

Frosted windows frame the scene,
Where our hopes and dreams convene.
The world outside, a canvas white,
While inside, sparks of love ignite.

Under blankets, side by side,
In this haven, hearts reside.
The pulse of winter, strong and clear,
Keeps us close, we hold so dear.

With every gust that drifts and sighs,
Life unfurls beneath gray skies.
In the quiet, spirits rise,
Finding warmth where love applies.

The Crystal Threshold

At dawn's light, the world transformed,
With crystal sheets, the earth adorned.
Nature's hush, a fragile sound,
In beauty's realm, serenity found.

Icicles hang like silver tears,
Reflecting thoughts, unspoken fears.
Walk the path with reverent care,
Touched by magic, light as air.

Every step a work of art,
Carved by winter, sweet and smart.
Frozen patterns, like a quilt,
Nature's canvas, love is built.

Beyond the threshold, worlds awake,
In icy breath, the heart may break.
But from the cold, new life will rise,
Emerging bright, beneath clear skies.

Weight of silence cannot bind,
As beauty moves, embracing mind.
Each moment, a crystal gaze,
In the stillness, hearts will blaze.

Frozen Time's Caress

In the stillness, moments freeze,
Gentle whispers brush the trees.
Time suspended, softly swirls,
Snowflakes weave in winter's pearls.

Every heartbeat echoes loud,
Draped in silence, like a shroud.
In this pause, where dreams collide,
Life's sweet secrets gently bide.

On frosted ground, the shadows play,
Carving figures, night and day.
In this hush, we find our place,
Wrapped in time's eternal grace.

The world beyond, a distant hum,
Yet here, it's peace that we become.
Silent journeys, we explore,
With every breath, we yearn for more.

Underneath the ice, a spark,
Fires of spring, within the dark.
Bound by winter's soft embrace,
We await the thaw's warm grace.

Frost Flowers on Ancient Stones

Frost blooms upon the ancient stones,
Whispers of winter, softened tones.
Crystals glistening in morning light,
Nature's artwork, pure and bright.

Silent gardens wrapped in white,
Memories linger, hidden from sight.
Each petal frozen, frozen in time,
Beauty captured in frigid rhyme.

Beneath the frost, the earth breathes slow,
Life waits patiently for spring's warm glow.
Eternal dance of cold and heat,
In cycles grand, they intertwine, meet.

Time weaves stories in every freeze,
Ancient stones hold secrets with ease.
Frost flowers bloom in the twilight's glow,
Silent sentinels, witnesses to snow.

The world holds still, in silence, enthralled,
As nature's canvas is gently sprawled.
Frost flowers whisper of days long past,
Their beauty fleeting, yet forever cast.

The Haunting Chill

A haunting chill drapes the weary town,
Shadows stretch long, and silence drowns.
Echoes of laughter fade into the night,
Veils of frost blocking all warmth and light.

Beware the whispers on the winter's breeze,
They carry secrets that never cease.
Footsteps lost in the fresh fallen snow,
Chilled by stories of those who won't go.

In the corners, figures flicker and fade,
Memories linger, their paths laid.
Under the moon, their presence feels near,
Wrapped in the silence, threaded with fear.

With every breath, the night deepens wide,
The chill beckons forth those long denied.
Frigid and eerie, time bends to their calls,
Remnants of lives behind those cold walls.

Yet in the silence, hope finds a way,
To thaw the hearts that winter can sway.
Though chill may haunt and shadows may creep,
The warmth of spring will put souls to sleep.

Lullabies Beneath the Ice

Lullabies drift beneath the ice,
Whispers of warmth, soft and concise.
Cradled in dreams where the winter sleeps,
Nature's heartbeat, the silence keeps.

Beneath the gelid grip of night,
Hidden melodies take flight.
Crystals hum with an ancient tune,
Starlit lullabies beneath the moon.

Remembered dances on frozen lakes,
Echoing soft, like childhood aches.
The cold wraps around, but love endures,
In tender moments, the heart ensures.

So let the snowflakes fall as they may,
In peaceful slumber, we softly lay.
Wrapped in dreams of spring's embrace,
A gentle promise, life interlace.

With every sigh, the world sleeps tight,
Lullabies echo through the shimmering night.
Beneath the ice, warmth waits to rise,
In whispered secrets, a new day lies.

Veils of Enchantment

Veils of enchantment drift through the trees,
Mystical whispers carried by the breeze.
A glimmering aura, soft and surreal,
Nature's own magic, a wondrous appeal.

Moonlight weaves through branches bare,
Casting shadows, light as air.
The world transformed, a dreamlike scene,
In twilight's glow, a realm between.

Stars ignite in the velvet sky,
Glimpses of realms that float nearby.
Gentle sighs weave through the night,
Echoes of magic, woven in light.

With every step taken on hallowed ground,
Enchantments whisper, secrets profound.
The earth feels alive, a pulsing heart,
In veils of wonder, each moment an art.

So take a breath, embrace the mystique,
In veils of enchantment, life feels unique.
For in the stillness, the mysteries call,
A dance of the ages, binding us all.

Rime-Kissed Twilight

The sky drapes low in hues of gray,
Whispers of dusk, the end of day.
Soft branches wear a diamond sheen,
In twilight's arms, a world serene.

Frosted fields in gentle repose,
As night's deep breath around us flows.
A hush envelops the waning light,
With dreams that dance in fading sight.

Stars peek through, like secrets shared,
Guardians of night, quietly paired.
In rime-kissed moments, hearts take flight,
Embracing the calm in soft twilight.

The moon ascends with silver grace,
Casting shadows, a timeless space.
Nature holds her breath in awe,
Lost in the beauty that we saw.

Time stands still as the world sleeps,
Wrapped in the stillness, nature keeps.
With each soft breath, the night unfolds,
A tale of wonder softly told.

In a Frost's Grasp

Morning breaks with a crystal glow,
Veils of frost on the earth below.
Each blade of grass a sparkling thread,
In winter's grip, all colors spread.

Whispers travel on a frosty breeze,
Nature dances among frozen trees.
Sunlight glints on a silver stream,
Casting shadows, a fleeting dream.

Birds sing soft in the morning's light,
Their melodies drift, a pure delight.
In the stillness, a world anew,
Where every moment feels like dew.

Footprints marked on a blanket white,
Tales of wanderers in flight.
Each step echoes through frosted fields,
Nature's bounty, the heart it yields.

The air so crisp, a breath of sighs,
Underneath the vast, azure skies.
In a frost's grasp, the world seems free,
A sacred space, just you and me.

Celestial Winter's Touch

Stars twinkle high in a velvet night,
Wrapped in warmth, the world feels right.
Snowflakes whisper on a gentle wind,
Tales of joy that winter has pinned.

Moonlight dances on a frozen lake,
Crafting shadows with each heartbeat's shake.
A world adorned in glistening white,
In celestial glow, everything's bright.

Frosted boughs sway in a solemn tune,
Serenading the softly glowing moon.
Each breath a cloud, a moment shared,
In winter's silence, souls declared.

Beneath the stars, dreams entwine,
As frosty tendrils trace the pine.
In this embrace, time drifts away,
Wrapped in the magic of winter's sway.

Celestial whispers map the skies,
Echoes of warmth, where beauty lies.
In the hush of night, we find our way,
Under winter's touch, forever stay.

Canvas of Snowbound Dreams

Glistening white, the world awaits,
A canvas bright with frozen gates.
Every flake a story told,
In whispers gentle, crisp and bold.

Footsteps mark the path we tread,
Through drifts of dreams where few have fled.
Each swirl and spin, a dance of grace,
Life painted on this winter's face.

Silent echoes fill the space,
Nature cradles us in soft embrace.
As stars conspire in darkened skies,
Hope glimmers bright, where magic lies.

Through snowbound realms, our spirits soar,
In every heart, a winter's lore.
Together we weave, hand in hand,
A tapestry across the land.

In snow's pure touch, we're intertwined,
Leaving behind the world unkind.
A canvas bright, our dreams now gleam,
In the embrace of snowbound dreams.

Chronicles of the Long Night

In shadows cast by the pale moon's glow,
Whispers of secrets begin to flow.
Stars flicker like memories half-remembered,
As the world sleeps, the darkness is tendered.

Time drifts slow like the night's soft breeze,
Echoes of stories told with ease.
The cold wraps close like a lover's embrace,
Holding the tales in a frozen space.

A distant howl breaks the silence deep,
The vigil of night bears vigil to keep.
Beneath the sky's vast, unending shroud,
Dreams dance through the quiet, both fierce and proud.

Each heartbeat marks the passage of time,
Moments unfold in rhythm and rhyme.
Chronicles weave in the depths of dusk,
Binding together the cool night's husk.

As dawn approaches, the shadows retreat,
Revealing the warmth in this chill they meet.
But echoes of night linger on the air,
A testament to the mysteries rare.

Beauty in the Frozen Silence

In the stillness where snowflakes dance,
A world awakens in silent romance.
Crystal glimmers on branches bright,
Nature's canvas, a pure delight.

Footprints left on the blanket white,
Stories unfold in the morning light.
Each breath hangs like a silent prayer,
Caught up in the magic that lingers there.

Whispers of beauty in the air so clear,
Soft melodies echo for those who hear.
Icicles hang like dreams turned real,
The heart finds peace in this frozen ideal.

Morning sun breaks through the horizon,
Awakening life where the ice has won.
Fields lie still, as if held in time,
Frozen silence, a perfect rhyme.

In every flake, a unique design,
Nature's wonder, a treasure divine.
Here in this moment, we pause and see,
Beauty thrives in frozen tranquility.

The Ghost of Winter's Whisper

In the hush of night, a chill takes flight,
The ghost of winter breathes soft and light.
Veils of frost lace the world in white,
Echoes of memories fade from sight.

Shadows linger where the pale winds moan,
As icy fingers grip the heart like stone.
Pines stand tall, a sentry so grand,
Guardians of secrets in this frostbitten land.

With every gust, a story is told,
Of warmth and joy, both brave and bold.
Yet whispers of sorrow in the midnight air,
Bring forth the ghosts that wander with care.

They dance through the night on a silver beam,
Flickering outlines like a distant dream.
A haunting reminder of seasons gone past,
The beauty of winter, so fleeting and vast.

In silence they linger, these spirits of frost,
Reminding us gently of the warmth that's lost.
Yet in their presence, we find peace and grace,
In the chilly embrace of winter's face.

The Journey of Icebound Dreams

Beyond the mountains where shadows sway,
Lie icebound dreams in their frozen play.
Crystals forming in the cold night's breath,
Holding the echoes of life and death.

Each step taken on the glittering floor,
Leads to realms where hopes can soar.
Beneath the surface, stories unfurl,
In the embrace of the winter whirl.

Shattered starlight in the depths below,
Bears witness to visions that flicker and glow.
In silence they whisper what's lost and won,
In these icebound dreams, both dark and fun.

A tale of longing, a quest for light,
Navigating paths veiled in the night.
To reach for warmth in the chill of despair,
The journey reveals what's truly rare.

So wander we must through this frozen terrain,
Where dreams are resilient, and hope won't wane.
With every heartbeat, we chase what's true,
In the land of ice, where dreams break through.

Beneath the Blanket of White

Softly falls the snow, so pure,
Covering all, a gentle lure.
Whispers dance from tree to tree,
In this silence, we are free.

Footprints trace a fleeting path,
Echoes of our winter's laugh.
In the stillness, dreams take flight,
Beneath the blanket of white.

A world transformed, bright and new,
Each flake holds a story true.
Laughter mingles with the chill,
As hearts embrace this winter thrill.

Clouds above drift slowly past,
In their shadows, memories cast.
Through the shimmer, visions gleam,
Wrapped in winter's cozy dream.

Here we linger, hand in hand,
In this frozen, wondrous land.
While the world around us sleeps,
Beneath the white, our promise keeps.

Chasers of Morning Light

Awake before the sun does rise,
We chase the dawn across the skies.
A canvas painted soft with hues,
In every moment, life renews.

With open hearts, we greet the day,
In golden beams, we find our way.
Each ray a blessing, warm and bright,
Guiding footsteps, chasers of light.

The morning dew glistens like jewels,
Nature's sparkle, nature's rules.
In every breath, the world awakes,
As night retreats, and daylight breaks.

Together we wander, side by side,
Through fields where dreams and hopes collide.
In laughter and joy, we unite,
Forever chasing morning light.

As shadows fade and colors blend,
Our spirits soar, our hearts extend.
In the embrace of dawn's delight,
We find our place in purest light.

Glacial Memories

In icy depths, the past resides,
Where frozen whispers softly glide.
Fractured time in shimmering forms,
A world transformed by winter storms.

Beneath the surface, tales unfold,
Of nature's wonders, brave and bold.
Each crystal's edge, a story spun,
Glacial memories, hushed but won.

We walk this path of ancient grace,
Each step reveals a quiet place.
Echoes of ages long since gone,
In the silence, their voices dawn.

Through frosty winds, we hear the call,
In nature's arms, we rise or fall.
With every breath, the ice will speak,
In glacial memories, strong yet weak.

So let us cherish, hold them dear,
These frozen moments, crystal clear.
For in their light, we find our way,
In the glacial dance, night meets day.

Night's Icy Cloak

Wrapped in shadows, cool and deep,
Night descends as the world sleeps.
With an icy cloak, it entwines,
A symphony of stars that shines.

Moonlight drapes the silent ground,
In the stillness, peace is found.
Whispers echo, soft and low,
As dreams ignite the depths below.

Each breath a cloud, each heartbeat spaced,
In night's embrace, fears are faced.
The chill sings lullabies to hearts,
In darkness, every soul imparts.

Through silver branches, shadows play,
Guiding us on this night's ballet.
In whispered tales, we find the spark,
That guides us through the velvet dark.

As dawn approaches, shadows yield,
Yet in the night, our spirits healed.
With gratitude, we greet the light,
For we have danced in night's icy cloak.

Fragments of a Blue Cornflower

Amidst the green, a spark so bright,
Petals dancing, catching light.
Its whispers tell of summer's grace,
In gentle winds, I find my place.

A delicate bloom sways with ease,
Each nod a tale carried by breeze.
Fragments of blue, a memory pure,
In nature's hands, I find my cure.

From garden paths to fields unknown,
Every step, a seed is sown.
A silent ode to moments past,
In every breath, a spell is cast.

Beneath the sky, where dreams entwine,
I trace the line where hearts align.
The blue cornflower, bold and true,
In its embrace, I start anew.

So let me linger in this glow,
Embracing all the love I know.
For in each fragment, life will bloom,
A tapestry of joy consumes.

A Tapestry of Icebound Memories

Frozen dreams on a winter's night,
Whispers echo in the pale moonlight.
Each snowflake glistens, a moment stored,
In a tapestry, memories adored.

Shadows dance on the icy floor,
Tales of laughter, forevermore.
Embroidered paths of love and loss,
Each stitch a sigh, each knot a cross.

With every breath, the cold embraces,
Hidden treasures in frozen places.
A tapestry woven with threads of time,
Where heartbeats linger, soft and chime.

Beneath the stars, I trace the seams,
In the chilly dark, I dream my dreams.
Woven tightly, in frost they stay,
Icebound memories, come what may.

So let the winter's tale unfold,
In every flake, a story told.
A tapestry of hearts entwined,
In the quiet, solace I find.

The Dance of Snowflakes

In twilight's hush, they swirl and sway,
Snowflakes twirl, a soft ballet.
Each one unique, a fleeting kiss,
In winter's arms, they find their bliss.

Whispers float on a crisp, cool breeze,
Dancing freely among the trees.
Silver threads woven in the air,
A delicate waltz, so sweet and rare.

They gather softly, a quilt of white,
Transforming the world in quiet night.
With grace they drift, a soft embrace,
Carving beauty in the stillness of space.

In every flurry, there's a spark,
Painting dreams in the chilly dark.
The dance goes on, as night turns dawn,
In winter's song, I'll be reborn.

So let them twirl, let them play,
Snowflakes whisper what words can't say.
In their dance, my heart takes flight,
Forever caught in winter's light.

Frosty Nocturne

Under a sky of inky hue,
Frosty whispers beckon anew.
The world is still, in slumber's hold,
A frosty nocturne, secrets told.

Crystals shimmer on the ground,
Nature's breath, a soft sound.
Moonlight glints on icy streams,
As night unfolds its silver dreams.

Footsteps echo on the frozen air,
A quiet comfort, with love to share.
Each moment a treasure, a soft embrace,
In the depths of winter's silent grace.

Where shadows play and echoes roam,
In this frosty realm, I feel at home.
With every heartbeat, a tale is spun,
In the embrace of the night, I run.

So let this nocturne guide my way,
Through frozen paths where memories lay.
In the chill, my spirit soars,
Frosty whispers, forever yours.

Echoes of a Silent Hearth

In shadows deep, the embers fade,
Whispers linger, memories made.
The crackling warmth now distant glow,
Time drifts softly, lost in slow.

Once we gathered, spirits bright,
Stories shared in the soft twilight.
Now the silence fills the air,
A hollow space where love laid bare.

Each flicker holds a secret sound,
In the silence, echoes found.
The past dances in amber light,
Yearning for a rekindled night.

With tender hearts, we reminisce,
The hearth's embrace, a gentle kiss.
Though quiet now, we'd still believe,
In every sigh, what we perceive.

For in the hush of memory's keep,
The echoes sing, as shadows creep.
A silent hearth can still ignite,
With love's pure flame, forever bright.

Veils of Winter's Breath

Frosted whispers drape the trees,
A world transformed by winter's ease.
Veils of white in silence spread,
Nature's song, so softly said.

The breath of chill wraps all around,
In sparkling hush, the peace is found.
Footsteps crunch on frozen ground,
Each sound a note, profound, unbound.

Stars above like diamonds shine,
In the cold, the heart aligns.
With every flake that falls in grace,
Winter's beauty finds its place.

The nights are long, the shadows deep,
Yet in the stillness, secrets sleep.
Veils of winter softly weave,
In dreams of warmth, we dare believe.

As dawn awakes with gentle light,
The icy grip begins to fight.
Yet in the heart, a promise glows,
Spring's tender touch, in time, bestows.

The Sparking Night's Spire

Starlit canopy, endless night,
Crickets sing in soft delight.
Moonbeams dance on whispered sighs,
The spire glows where mystery lies.

In twilight's arms, the shadows play,
Chasing echoes till the break of day.
The wind, a tale of far-off shores,
Invites the soul to dream once more.

Glimmers twinkle, wishes soar,
Every spark, a hope restored.
The silence hums with cosmic tune,
An ancient song beneath the moon.

Beneath the night's enchanting dome,
Each heart is drawn, a sunken home.
We gather dreams in starlit jars,
And fill our souls with guiding stars.

As dawn whispers its golden thread,
Leaving sprightly evening's bed,
The night recedes with all its fire,
But lingers still, the sparking spire.

Veils of the Midnight Sky

In shadows deep, the midnight sighs,
A tapestry of muted cries.
Stars like jewels, scattered bright,
Veils of dreams take sudden flight.

Clouds drift softly, curtains drawn,
Hiding secrets until dawn.
The moon, a guardian, watches low,
Illuminating paths we know.

Gentle winds weave silent tunes,
Caressing leaves beneath the moons.
Whispers float on evening's breath,
Carrying tales of life and death.

In every glow, a story spins,
Of lost loves and where it begins.
Veils of night, a soft embrace,
Cradle moments, time and space.

Yet as the sun begins to rise,
The midnight fades, a sweet surprise.
Though veils may part, we'll hold them near,
In starlit hearts, they linger here.

Whispers of Winter's Embrace

Snowflakes dance in silent air,
Blankets white, so soft and rare.
Whispers weave through frosty trees,
Nature's hush, a tender breeze.

Footprints trace a path of gold,
Stories of the brave, the bold.
Winter's heart beats strong and slow,
In its arms, the world seems glow.

Moonlight spills on sparkling ground,
Every shadow makes a sound.
Whirling winds and glimmering glow,
In this calm, all spirits flow.

Hushed whispers of the ancient night,
Crystals sparkle, pure delight.
Snowflakes fall like whispered dreams,
Wrapped in warmth, or so it seems.

In the stillness, magic grows,
Winter's wonder, subtle shows.
Embrace the chill, let it stay,
Whispers guide the heart's ballet.

Glacial Breath

A breath of ice upon the lake,
Glistening shores that silence break.
Whispers echo from the deep,
Secrets that the glaciers keep.

Frosted whispers kiss the night,
Moonbeams dance in silver light.
Air so crisp, it clears the mind,
In its chill, peace we can find.

Mountains wear their tattered white,
Guardians of an ancient rite.
Glacial breath, a fleeting prayer,
Calling forth the dreams we share.

Time stands still, as moments freeze,
In the grasp of biting breeze.
Nature's canvas, stark and bright,
Portraits painted in the night.

Breath of winter, strong and pure,
In this place, our hearts endure.
Glacial whispers, soft and clear,
Guide us gently, year by year.

Shimmering Frost on Ebon Leaves

Ebon leaves, adorned with frost,
Silent beauty, never lost.
Shimmering in the morning light,
Each a gem, a pure delight.

Beneath the sky so vast and gray,
Nature's art is here to stay.
Whispers of a world reborn,
In the chill of winter's morn.

Morning dew, like diamonds strewn,
Sparkles softly, catching noon.
In the quiet, whispers play,
Through the leaves in dance ballet.

Branches sway in gentle sighs,
Answering the winter cries.
Frosted whispers spin and weave,
In the heart of autumn's eve.

Beauty lies in fading light,
Tiny wonders, brief in flight.
Nature's brush paints in silence,
Finding peace in chill's embrace.

The Quietude of Chilled Mornings

In the dawn, a tranquil hush,
Nature stirs without a rush.
Chilled air breathes a frosty song,
A symphony that feels so strong.

Birds awake with gentle coos,
Whispers mingling with the blues.
Softly falling, leaves descend,
In this moment, time can bend.

Sunrise paints the world anew,
Colors bright breaking through.
Quietude wraps the waking land,
In its grasp, we understand.

Crystalline branches catch the light,
Each a diamond, pure and bright.
Nature holds her breath, in pause,
Echoing the world's applause.

Chilled mornings bring a sacred peace,
In the stillness, hearts release.
Let us wander through this grace,
In winter's arms, we find our place.

The Awakening of White

In the hush of morning light,
Snowflakes dance in pure delight,
Each flake a whisper, soft and bright,
Nature's canvas, clothed in white.

Silence swells, the world holds breath,
A blanket shrouds the fields in death,
Yet life stirs softly underneath,
As blooms prepare to conquer death.

The trees stand tall, their crowns aglow,
Beneath the weight of icy show,
Branches bow, yet still they grow,
In winter's grasp, they find their flow.

Footsteps echo on the frozen ground,
Where peace and stillness can be found,
A tranquil voice, without a sound,
In this awakening all is crowned.

The sun peeks through, a golden ray,
Kissing the frost, in warm display,
Life reawakens, chasing gray,
In the heart of winter's sway.

When Stars Bear the Chill

Beneath a sky of endless night,
Stars shimmer with a chilly light,
Each twinkle speaks of distant flight,
A cosmic dance, cold and bright.

Whispers of frost in the still air,
Moonlight glimmers, soft and rare,
Nature's breath, a silvery flare,
In the calm, a world laid bare.

The night holds secrets close to heart,
In the shadows, dreams depart,
A chill creeps in, yet warms the art,
Of wonder spun like fragile chart.

When stars bear witness to our fears,
They sparkle with the weight of years,
Stories told through silent tears,
A universe that often steers.

In the depths of this endless blue,
We find a peace, profound and true,
Chilled by beauty, spirits renew,
As stars reflect the inner view.

Perceptions of the Icy Realm

In the realm of frost and ice,
Where frozen dreams and whispers slice,
Each breath a cloud, a fleeting vice,
In stillness lies a great entice.

The crystalline world, a fractured glass,
Reflections shimmer as moments pass,
Perceptions shift, like shadows cast,
A tapestry of dreams amassed.

Mountains cloaked in white embrace,
Glistening peaks, a frozen grace,
In icy depth, we find our place,
As nature paints with softest trace.

A quiet stroll on nature's trail,
Every step a crisp inhale,
Resonating like a gentle gale,
Whispers echo, soft yet pale.

In this realm, the spirit soars,
With every flake, the heart restores,
In icy wonders, life implores,
A beauty found that ever pours.

Beneath the Tides of Frost

Underneath the silent sea,
Frozen waves, a mystery,
Life suspended, yet to be,
In icy depths, tranquility.

Ripples freeze as currents slow,
Where shadows dance, and secrets flow,
In the silence, life will grow,
Underneath the quiet glow.

The tide withdraws, revealing grace,
An ocean's calm, a soft embrace,
Each frozen treasure finds its place,
In nature's realm, a poet's space.

Above, the world is wrapped in chill,
While below, a dance of will,
Creatures thrive, time stands still,
In depths of frost, the heart will fill.

Amidst the ice, hope finds its way,
Beneath the frosty waves, we sway,
In silent tides where dreams convey,
A world reborn at break of day.

Elysian Cold

In a realm where silence sings,
The snowflakes dance, on gossamer wings.
Each breath released, a cloud of mist,
Whispers of winter, a ghostly tryst.

Trees adorned in crystal lace,
Nature wears a frozen face.
The twilight glows, a soft embrace,
In Elysian lands, we find our place.

Footsteps muffled, dreams abound,
In this quiet, peace is found.
Stars shimmer in the chilly night,
As hearts ignited, burn so bright.

Glistening paths and trails anew,
Beneath the sky, so vast and blue.
In frozen fields where hope is sown,
We gather warmth, though all seems stone.

The warmth we share, a light so bold,
Chasing shadows, breaking cold.
With every laugh, and every sigh,
In Elysian cold, we learn to fly.

Tapestries of Ice and Light

Fractured beams through frosty panes,
A world adorned with silvery chains.
Each droplet caught in beams so bright,
Woven tales of ice and light.

Whispers swirl in crystalline air,
Secrets held in winter's care.
Colors shift in dawn's soft kiss,
Nature's magic, an icy bliss.

Mountains rise like sentinels proud,
Beneath their gaze, we gather crowd.
Palaces of frost, intricately planned,
A wonderland beneath our hand.

The moonlit spark dances with grace,
In every corner, a silent space.
Here, tales of the past ignite,
In tapestries of icy light.

Beneath the stars, we spin our dreams,
In the cool embrace of winter's themes.
With every breath, the magic's near,
In harmony, we sing and cheer.

Glistening Echoes of Winter

Across the land, a blanket deep,
Nature's lullaby, a timeless sleep.
Glistening echoes in shimmering white,
Winter's canvas, pure and bright.

Crystal rivers, silent streams,
Reflecting glows of distant dreams.
Each touch of snow, a soft caress,
In winter's arms, we find our rest.

Frosted branches sway with ease,
Whispering secrets in the breeze.
With every flake, the stories unfold,
Of warmth within, though chill takes hold.

Caverns of ice, in caves they dwell,
Tell tales of beauty, where magic fell.
Beneath the stars, the world seems bright,
In glistening echoes, hearts take flight.

Together we roam, side by side,
Through winter's wonder, our hearts abide.
In frosty realms, our spirits soar,
Glistening echoes, forever more.

The Enchantment of Deep Freeze

Silent whispers in the air,
A frosty spell, a magic rare.
In deep freeze, where shadows play,
Hearts entwined, come what may.

Icicles hang like frozen dreams,
In the stillness, softly gleams.
Nature's breath, a chilled refrain,
In every flake, a sweetened pain.

Footsteps crunch on paths of white,
Under the glow of silvery light.
Each moment savored, time stands still,
In the enchantment, we feel the thrill.

Wandering through this mystic haze,
Lost in wonder, caught in a daze.
Hand in hand, we face the night,
In deep freeze, our souls ignite.

As dawn breaks with colors bright,
The world awakens, a wondrous sight.
In every heart, winter's truth,
The enchantment flows, eternal youth.

Milton Keynes UK
Ingram Content Group UK Ltd.
UKHW010229111224
452348UK00011B/622